STRESS RELIEVING

WEEEEE BOOK'S

The Green Book!

Mandalas

Wendy Pikys

Dear artist:

Choose a model that inspires you, select the tools and prepare a quiet place.

If you wish you can play soft music, or light some scented candles or an incense stick.

If you think you need help to exteriorize your emotions, we suggest you color from the inside out.

If you are on an inner quest, for affirmation or self-knowledge, paint from the outside in on the design.

namaste

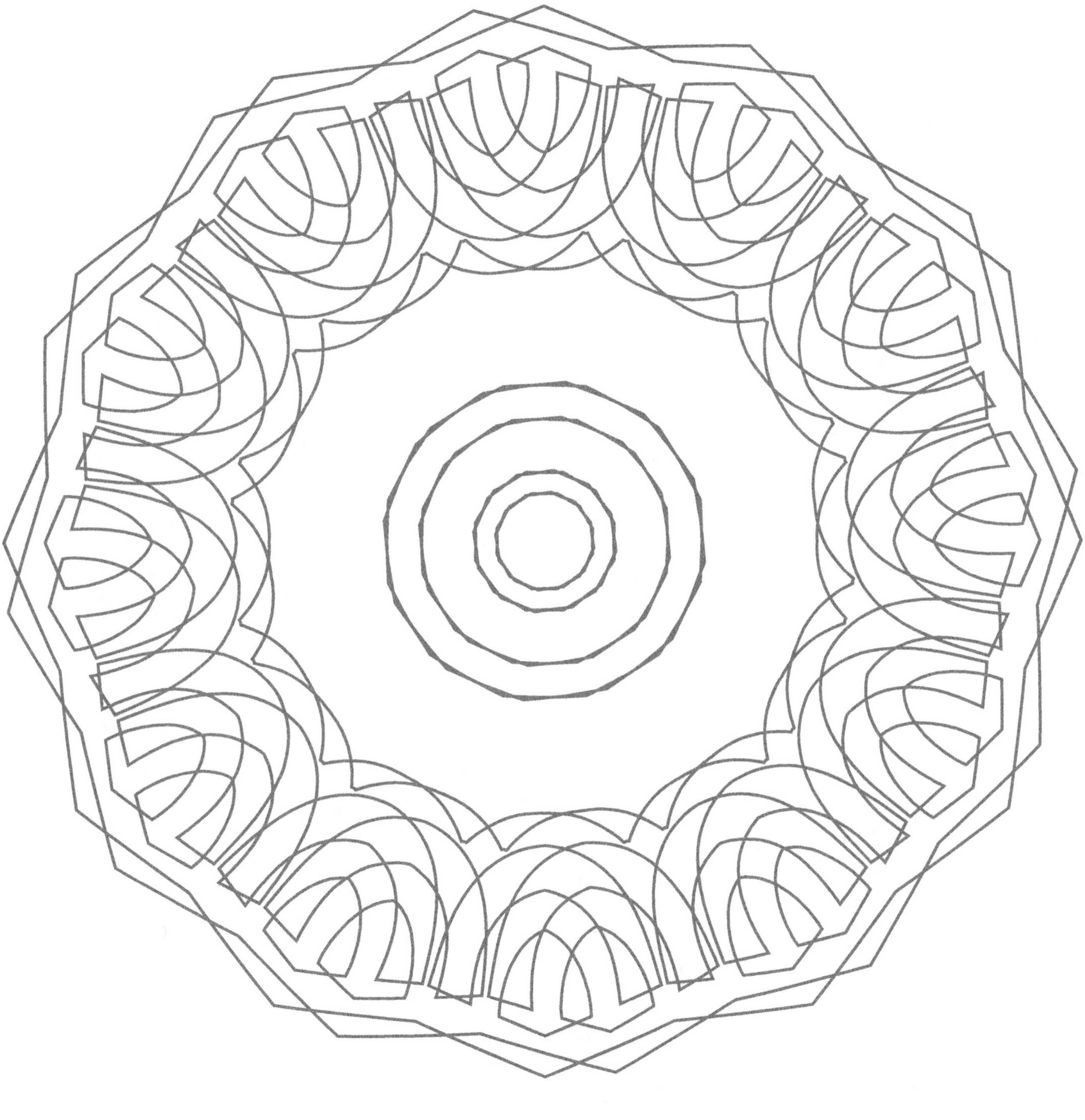

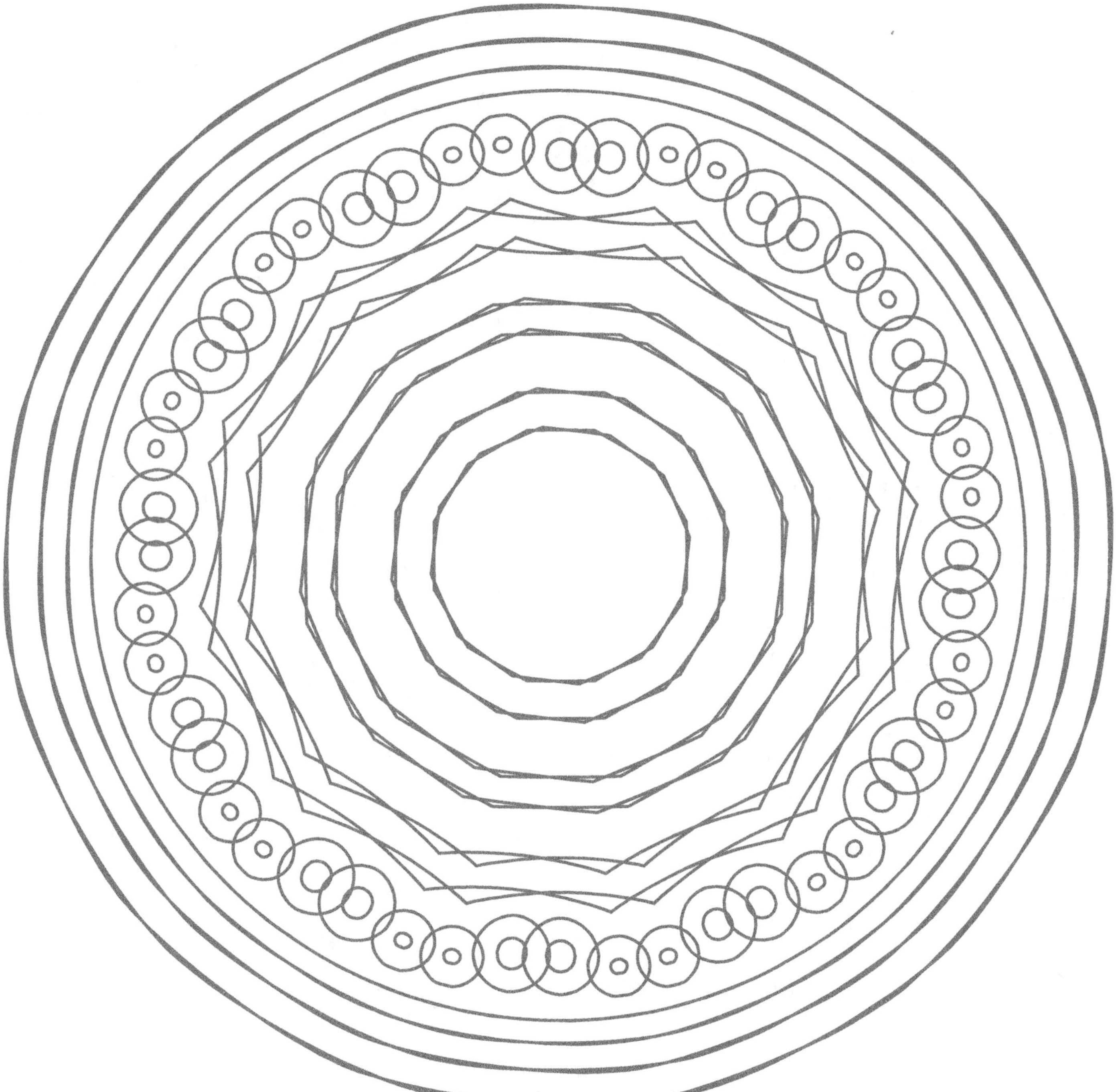

WEEEEE BOOK'S

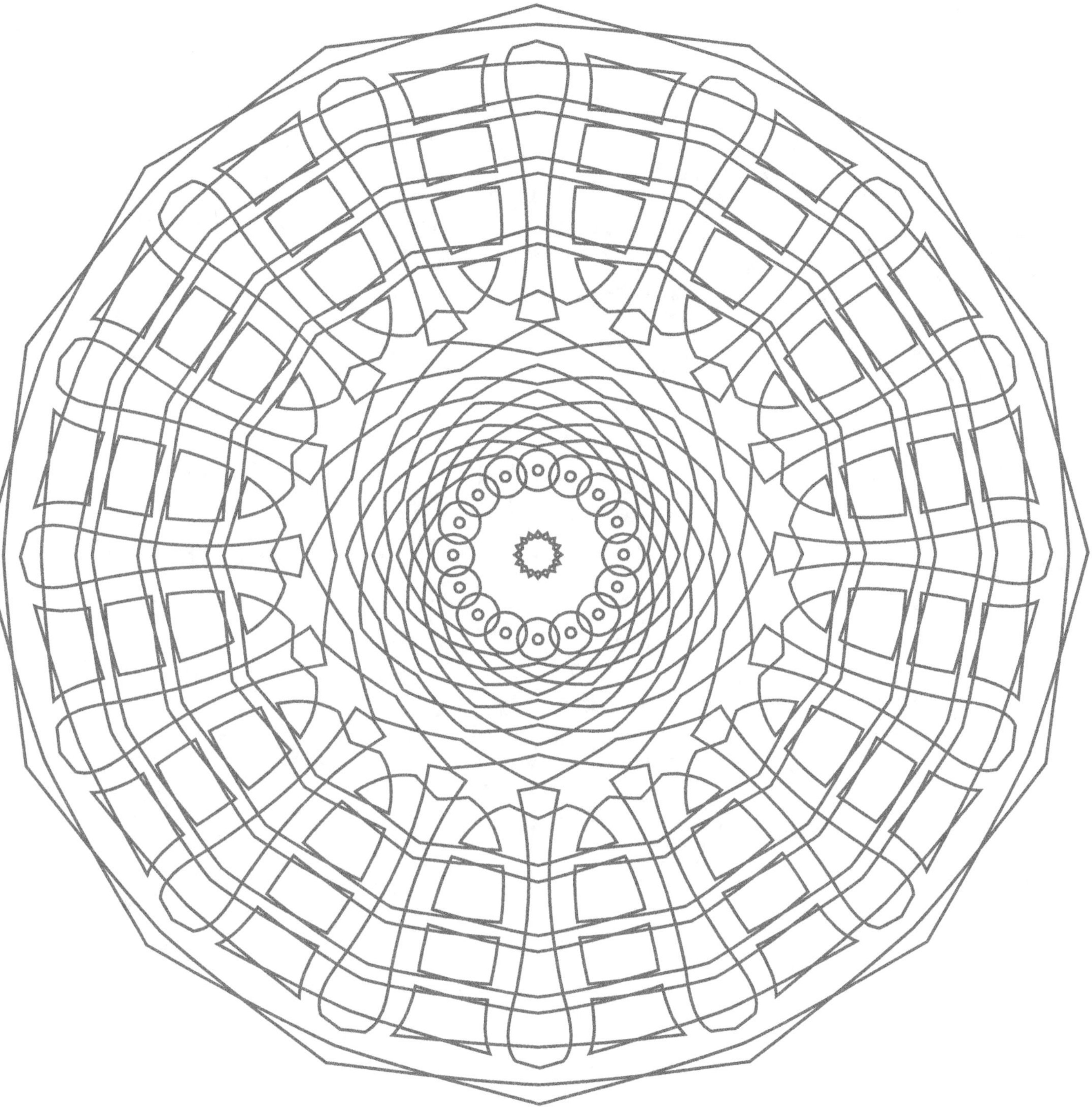

WEEEEE BOOK'S

The Green Book!

By Wendy Pikys

Mandala is a word of Sanskrit origin and means 'circle'; it represents the unity, harmony and infinity of the universe. It represents the unity, harmony and infinity of the universe.

www.ingramcontent.com/pod-product-compliance
Lightning Source LLC
Chambersburg PA
CBHW081413250726
48654CB00013B/1690
* 9 7 9 8 6 8 8 9 3 5 3 6 3 *